FOLK ART OF MEXICO

GERD DÖRNER

FOLK ART OF MEXICO

With 28 color plates
Translated by Gladys Wheelhouse

NEW YORK: A. S. BARNES AND CO.

Published by

A. S. Barnes and Co. Inc.
8 East 36th Street
New York 16, N.Y.

© 1962 by Wilhelm Andermann Verlag, Munich.
Printed in Germany.

I wish to express my thanks to the many friends and authorities on Mexican folk-art who kindly helped me with information and advice, and in particular to Dr. Daniel F. Rubin de la Borbolla, the Director of the Museo de Artes e Industrias Populares de Mexico, Mrs. Irmgard Weitlaner-Johnson of the Instituto Nacional Indigenista, Mrs. Carmen Cook de Leonard of the Centro de Investigaciones Antropologicas de Mexico, as well as to Mr. Victor Fosado jr. and Mr. José Luis Franco.

Mexican folk-art is not easy to understand, for its forms of expression are extremely manifold, and its roots and derivations are numerous and diverse. In its origin it dates from the ancient Indian cultures, and many forms of expression still found today can be traced back to these cultures. The Spanish conquerors of the country influenced it very considerably, and there are certain indications that its character was to some extent also determined by wares from the Far East which were introduced into the country through trading media that have so far never been clarified.

Nowadays other influences already play a part in determining the character of Mexican folk-art in the more accessible regions of the country: the process of disintegration as a result of the modernization of life, industrial production, and the indiscriminate demand on the part of many tourists for souvenirs are all decisive factors in this respect.

The history of art has naturally occupied itself above all with the fascinating story of the ancient pre-Hispanic cultures and has, relatively speaking, neglected the folk-art of the country. Authorities on the subject of the American continent stress again and again, however, that no other country there possesses so manifold and rich a folk-art as Mexico. But unfortunately the authors who have made a more intensive study of Mexican folk-art are few in number, and, moreover, they wrote their works in the days when vast regions of the country were still inaccessible. Only during the past fifteen years have most parts of Mexico become easily accessible. Hence there are certain gaps in the information available on its folk-art, for in many cases it has proved impossible to trace individual features back to their initial stage.

The Country and its Inhabitants

The territory of the Republic of Mexico has an area of 760,579 sq. miles, that is to say it is eight times as large as the Federal Republic of Germany. The climate in the individual regions of the country varies greatly owing to the considerable differences in altitude, which range from sea-level to more than 6,000 feet. The capital, which has a population of 4 million, is situated at a height of 6,600 feet, whilst 20 per cent of the area of the country has an altitude ranging between 3,000 and 4,500 feet, and 30 per cent an altitude between 4,500 and 6,000 feet and over. The population today numbers about 30 million, of which (according to the statistics of 1940) 5.5 million are pure Indians. According to the same statistics, 35.5 per cent of the total number of American Indians live in Mexico.

By the end of the Spanish colonization era the pure Indian population of Mexico, according to various statistics, had dwindled to 2–3 million. This figure shows how small the national group actually was which transmitted the old, traditional foundations of Mexican folk-art to posterity. And in those fields of folk-art which owe their characteristic features or, in fact, their earliest beginnings to the Spanish conquerors of the country, the craftsmen are as a rule Indians or mestizos. If one compares the size of this relatively small and much divided national group with the far larger peoples of East Asia, for instance, one cannot help but admire the achievements of Mexican folk-art.

The Early History of the Country

No doubt what strikes one most about the early history of Mexico is the fact that there existed – probably as a result of the vastness of the country – a number of ancient cultures, partly one after another and partly side by side, and some of them achieved a high degree of excellence. With but a few exceptions, most of the knowledge which our modern era has of these ancient cultures is more or less only fragmentary and is based mainly on the excavations carried out by archaeologists.

The more recent history of Latin America begins in the 15th and 16th centuries with the Spanish invasion, and of Mexico with the landing of

Mexican Pottery

In the background a raffia mat typical of Mexico. On a sarape woven in León, in the back row (from left to right), two large basins used for preparing food, both of them made in Metepec. The larger one has a diameter of over 2 feet. Between them a pitcher from Tepakan / Campeche. In the second row: a pitcher from Toliman / Guerrero, a copper dish and a jug from Santa Clara del Cobre / Michoacan, as well as jugs from Tonatico / Mexico, Amayaltepec / Guerrero, and Amatenango del Valle / Chiapas. In the row in front: a copper dish from Santa Clara del Cobre, earthenware dishes and plates from the district of San Miguel Allende / Guanajuato, Puebla (in the Talavera style), and Tzintzuntzan / Michoacan, with a cream-coloured background. The large green plate in the centre of the front row comes from Patamban / Michoacan, the plate on the left from Tzintzuntzan (probably copied from the style of Patamban), the plate on the right from Coroéo / Guanajuato.

Fernando Cortez in 1519. One by one the existing realms and cultures were destroyed. This urge to destroy on the part of the conquerors, which was prompted by religious motives, has deprived us of much information on the way of thinking and living of these ancient peoples, so that we know less about relatively later eras in their culture than we do about much older cultural epochs in East Asia.

THE ANCIENT CULTURES OF MEXICO

Before we pass on to our actual subject we should like to say something about the ancient cultures of the country, for it seems fitting at this point to mention in brief, at least, the earliest historical and cultural influences on which the later folk-art of Mexico was based. For a considerable period of time the various styles of these ancient cultures influenced Mexican folk-art and some of these influences are still apparent today.

Of the various races which peopled Mexico in earliest times, the *Aztecs* (who inhabited the region of the present capital and its surrounding districts) were the most famous. Since their realm was the first to be conquered by the Spanish invaders, we can today still form a fairly clear picture of their mode of living. The highest cultural level was probably attained by the "Hellenes" of Mexico, the *Mayas*, who migrated from Guatemala to the region now known as the state of Yucatan.

The mountainous region was inhabited by the *Chichimecs* and the *Toltecs,* who settled in Tula but later conquered the region of Yucatan. Before their time there existed the ancient culture of *Teotihuacan,* symbolized by its majestic pyramid, which was even larger than those to be found in Egypt. The *Olmecs* inhabited the southern part of the state now known as Veracruz. The huge stone sculptures and, in particular, the stone heads, which are over 6 feet high, that bear witness to the culture of the Olmecs are still a mystery to our modern age. Some of the other outstanding cultures of the country can probably be traced back to this early civilization.

In the north of the same state there were the *Totonacs*, and still further north, on the site of the present Tampico, the *Huastecs,* who, together with the Mayas, created the most exquisite stone sculptures in ancient Mexico.

Earthenware Figures for a Christmas Candelabra, from Metepec / Mexico

Earthenware candelabras over 3 feet high and usually decorated with Christmas motifs depicting the story of the Birth of Christ and various scenes to the Flight into Egypt, are made in Metepec / Mexico. The basic shape of the candelabras is fashioned by hand, the figures, as in the pre-Hispanic technique, are made with the aid of small earthenware moulds. (Raul Kamffer Collection)

The *Mixtecs* and the *Zapotecs* inhabited the region of the present state of Oaxaca, whilst the northwest region of the country, along the Pacific coast, was peopled by the *Tarascans*.

VARIOUS INFLUENCES ON MEXICAN FOLK-ART

The manifold variety of these ancient cultures, which we have only mentioned in brief, naturally influenced the folk-art, though in many cases this influence was only local. After the conquest of the country, however, this folk-art was exposed to many Spanish and, above all in architecture, to Moorish influences. The new materials and techniques introduced by the Spaniards enabled the native craftsmen to achieve a higher degree of perfection as regards forms of expression.

The Spaniards taught the Mexicans how to obtain and use wool, glass and iron; they also introduced glazing and fine leatherwork, two crafts which were entirely new to Mexico. Horses were likewise a Spanish innovation, and in those days the native inhabitants fled in terror at the sight of them. Today, however, the Mexicans rank amongst the best equestrians in the world. An account of the manufacture of all the essentials, such as riding-dress and equipment, which are part of Mexican horsemanship, would, in fact, fill a whole book.

Other influences from an entirely different direction, namely from China, are said to have penetrated to those regions where the predominant craft was and still is lacquering. Archaeological finds, however, would appear to indicate that this craft originated in the country itself.

On the other hand, it must be borne in mind that all the former branches of folk-art which had served cultural and religious needs were for the most part destroyed as a result of the Spanish conquest of the country. The ancient peoples were deprived of their rulers, their culture and their gods; thus the preconditions for the higher forms of expression of the original folk-art were eliminated. Objects of art and culture, luxury articles, and in particular clothes and objects used in everyday life were now completely influenced by the Spanish style. The exquisite craft of featherwork, in which the valuable plumage of tropical birds was used to make the robes of the tribal kings, continued to survive for a time in the creation of pictures.

A Censer from Oaxaca

During the night of All Souls copal is burnt in censers whilst the families of the departed sit by the graves. In the region of the Zapotecs in the state of Oaxaca these censers are still fashioned in the same shape as they were hundreds of years ago. The figures which adorn the rim of the censer symbolize the souls of the dead, who, according to an old Mexican belief, return to the living once a year, during the night of All Souls.

When the term "folk-art" first came to be used, the average outsider who regarded himself as a superior civilized being in an era which deemed itself "progressive" had no longer any spiritual contact with the primitive powers of expression of the people. What indeed was "folk-art", as we now designate it? It was merely the desire on the part of a people or tribe that was awakening culturally to beautify objects used in daily life and in religious cults and to give them a character of their own by using the various materials and handicraft skills available. This desire was not however prompted by any conscious intention or consideration but solely by the artistic creativeness which every inventive and skilled craftsman possesses. And on the whole the basic forms of such objects have retained their essential features throughout thousands of years. For it is precisely a fascinating characteristic of folk-art that it usually prefers "utility" forms. Thus many wares of the potter's craft today differ very little in form from those that were created in earliest times. And early religious motifs of the pre-Hispanic era are still apparent in many of the wares created today. A change was usually effected by a new design of ornamentation, and once such a change had met with the approval of customers, it was retained in future. The inventiveness of the Mexicans as regards new variations of designs has always been inexhaustible.

Apart from certain technical innovations introduced by the Spaniards, the Indian craftsman still uses various techniques which date from earliest times. Even today most Mexican potters still make their wares without using a potter's wheel and do not fashion them by hand but press them out in moulds, a technique which was applied by the earliest potters when making the figures of the ancient deities of the pre-Hispanic era. The Mexican craftsman has always been responsive to new, stimulating ideas, but once he has mastered the style and technique and is allowed a free hand in his work, he imbues these ideas with his own designs. And in this respect he certainly reveals an amazing and unique imagination.

The following experience of a manager of a tile-works is typical of Mexico. He requested the foreman to make some samples with various designs on them in order to show them to prospective customers. Within a couple of days the foreman and his hands turned out 800 tiles, every one

Earthenware Figure of Death, from Metepec / Mexico

To mark the occasion of All Souls, death is represented in many different forms. As toys, as cartoons, in the form of confectionery and in countless earthenware objects. This conception of death and the life beyond is certainly unusual and is not found amongst any other peoples. (Raul Kamffer Collection)

of them with a different design. This classical description of the mentality of the Indian craftsmen is to be found in a story by B. Traven, who is however regarded with a certain animosity in Mexico.

VARIOUS FORMS OF EXPRESSION OF MEXICAN FOLK-ART

Pottery

Since earliest times man's thoughts have always been occupied in the first place with the question of obtaining food, a roof over his head, and clothes, and then, secondly, with the utensils in which to store and prepare his food. In prehistoric days man wore the skins of the animals that he hunted and killed, and he used the husks of certain fruits as utensils, a habit which is still in evidence today amongst numerous primitive peoples. But it was no doubt man's desire to possess utensils even in earliest times which led to the development of pottery as one of the oldest crafts.

As regards this type of folk-art Mexico has an ancient and highly developed tradition; indeed, it is quite impossible to estimate the amount of pre-Hispanic pottery which has been discovered, or which still lies buried in various regions of the country. In spite of the modern mass-production of household utensils which has also become customary in Mexico, the potter's craft is still predominant there, and the wares produced are certainly unique in their variety of designs and styles. Many of them are of such excellent quality that they can be used in the modern home since they are fireproof.

This craft is practised in those regions where the soil contains deposits of suitable clay. As in pre-Hispanic days, the finished wares are transported from some districts over vast distances – in former days by donkeys – to the markets. Certain places known for their particularly high-grade or unique pottery are mentioned below.

The various forms and shapes of the wares are determined by their different uses. One of the most typical utensils found here is the round pitcher. Above the centre of gravity there are three holes, through which a rope is passed, by means of which the pitcher is carried. Since droughts are a com-

A Money-box from Tonala near Guadalajara

Many of the villages in the vicinity of Guadalajara are still important pottery centres. The pottery made in Tonala is most unique. The surface of this brightly painted money-box, in the form of a pig, is not glazed; before the designs were painted on it, it was polished with stones until it acquired a dull gloss. (Ceramics Museum, Tlaquepaque)

mon occurrence in many parts of the country, thousands of families are often obliged to carry their water supplies over long distances. Dishes and basins used for preparing food are usually large in size, and some of them have a diameter of 3 feet and more. In the district of Guadalajara earthenware bathtubs were formerly made. And according to figures ascertained by Dr. Atl, there were 4,000 potters' families in the Republic of Mexico in 1922.

The most important pottery centres are situated in the states of Mexico, Jalisco, Oaxaca, Michoacan, Puebla, Guanajuato, Hidalgo, Aguascalientes, Tlaxcala, San Luis Potosi, Chiapas and Chihuahua. Since there are more than 500 pottery centres, it is impossible to describe all the different styles and designs in detail, but the following brief survey will give the reader some idea of their great variety.

In certain regions, some of which only became accessible in comparatively recent years whilst others are still practically inaccessible, many of the old shapes, designs and patterns have been retained to this day. This is on the whole the case in the mountainous districts of Michoacan, San Luis Potosi, Morelos and Puebla. Toliman, Amayaltepec and Umpango in the state of Guerrero are noted in particular for their light-coloured pottery, on which animal and flower motifs and other ornamental designs are painted in brown colours before the clay is baked. In Chiapas and especially in Amatenango del Valle the designs are more primitive. But in Tapacan, in the plain of Campeche, we also find similar and more ornate designs. Who knows, – perhaps the artistic influence of the Mayas is still expressed in these designs? Whilst the town of Oaxaca is famed for its glazed pottery decorated with flower motifs, San Bartolo Coyotepec a few miles away is noted for its black pottery ware, which is still produced by an ancient technique. Numerous shapes depicting animals, mermaids, and bells, etc., are pressed with the aid of moulds. Many of these toys are provided with a whistle, a custom which dates from the pre-Hispanic era and for which no explanation has so far been found. Old customs and traditions have also served as a model for some of the light-coloured pottery ware, including the shapes of animals produced in Santa Maria Atzompa, but the green glaze used for some parts of these shapes is a more recent innovation.

The ware produced in the town of Puebla is particularly outstanding on account of its artistic quality. Up to 1650 the style of Talavera in Spain was faithfully copied down to the smallest detail. After the liberation the

*Earthenware Vessel decorated with Floral and Animal Motifs,
from Tonala near Guadalajara*

The finely drawn floral and animal motifs on this vessel are under the glazed
surface. (Ceramics Museum, Tlaquepaque)

potters and tile-makers continued to use the standard colours blue, white and yellow, but they now gave their products a characteristic style and quality of their own.

Mention must also be made of the pottery centres in the vicinity of Guadalajara, above all Tonalá and Tlaquepaque. Two different processes are used in Tonalá; in the first, a process usually applied when making animal shapes, the clay is baked twice after its surface has been smoothed so carefully with the aid of stones that it almost appears to be glazed. In the second process, the clay is decorated with highly artistic animal and flower designs and is then baked twice and glazed. The first of these two processes was, incidentally, also used in olden days when making bathtubs. Exquisite pottery ware is produced in Tlaquepaque. But unfortunately this craft has been commercialized here to an alarming extent and, in order to satisfy modern mass tastes, now concentrates to a large extent on the production of large vases bearing "Chinese designs", which are however not based on an old tradition but are a recent innovation introduced about 10 to 15 years ago.

A typical example of the creation of new styles in recent times is the pottery ware of Tzintzuntzan on Lake Patzcuaro in the state of Michoacan. About 20 years ago a woman-potter from Morelia came to live there and began to make ware which had a yellow background decorated with crude designs in brown, depicting scenes from life on the shores of the lake and fishing motifs. Today the style of the Tzintzuntzan pottery is known throughout the entire country, but most people are not aware of its recent origin.

And at this point I should like to narrate a little story told to me by the patron of this woman-potter. Some friends of Picasso sent the famous painter some Tzintzuntzan pottery ware, no doubt because it somewhat resembles his modern style in certain features. He wrote a most enthusiastic letter addressed to the "honoured master". But the poor woman was unable to appreciate his praise since she probably did not even know who Picasso was. Today one can still buy her wares for a few pence.

Other types of pottery also include vessels used in religious cults. In many districts, for instance, earthenware censers, which are used on All Souls day, are made; the most exquisite ones are those designed in the Zapotec style, which are produced in the state of Oaxaca. Finally, mention must also be

Earthenware Toys and Vessels

It is impossible to enumerate the various types of earthenware toys and figures.
On a rare and beautiful sarape, worn on festive occasions by the Mayo Indians in
the mountainous districts of the state of Sonora, from left to right in the back
row, a black painted horse from Acatlan / Puebla, with pitchers suspended from
its back, and a jug shaped like a duck and designed in the pre-Hispanic style, from
Ocotlan / Puebla. In the middle row, a dog – fashioned in the shape used in
earliest times – which, together with two other dogs, is used to support the large
earthenware dishes in which the tortillas are heated. These shapes are still found
in the Sierra de Puebla, in particular in Cuetzalan. The little figure of the bread-
vendor comes from Tlaquepaque near Guadalajara. The horse painted in various
colours comes from Acatlan / Puebla. In the front row, the figure of an angel, used
as a candlestick, from the state of Guerrero, and a black earthenware dog from
Coyotepec / Oaxaca. There is a whistle in its tail.

made of the "trees of life", a customary wedding present in Mexico. The most famous and most beautiful ones are made in Metepec in the state of Mexico and in Izucar de Matamoros in the State of Puebla. They are decorated with numerous figures and animals and rank as the finest creations of the art of pottery in Mexico today. They are, however, a comparatively recent innovation, for they only became known at the beginning of this century. They are shaped like candelabras and some of them are over three feet high. According to the season of the year, motifs referring to Easter or Christmas are used.

Many of the old deities whose images can still be seen today in the famous, ancient Mexican temples are also reproduced – some of them most exquisitely – in various types of pottery.

Textiles

When considering this branch of folk-art one must distinguish between local costumes and the textiles which are used more or less throughout the whole country. In this respect sarape-weaving plays an important part, since it is either locally centralized, or else extends over vast regions of the country.

What are the typical features of the local costumes? The attire worn by the menfolk has always been fairly plain and on the whole devoid of ornamental accessories: a white shirt, white trousers, leather-plaited sandals, and a sombrero, a broad-brimmed straw hat which varies in shape very considerably from district to district. The outstanding exceptions as regards the men's attire are the Huicholes, a small tribe in the state of Nayarit, whose local costume is beautifully embroidered, and the mountain-tribes in the state of Chiapas, who wear "tzotziles" and "tzeltales".

The typical costume of the womenfolk, which is still worn today by the Chinantecas, Mazatecas, Yalaltecas and other tribes of the state of Oaxaca, as well as by the Maya women, has always been the "huipil", a loose sack reaching to the waist, to the knees or below, and worn with or without an underskirt according to its length. Whereas the "huipiles" worn by the Maya women are lavishly embroidered with flower motifs and reveal a strong Spanish influence, those worn by the tribes of the state of Oaxaca

A Huichol Indian from the Mountains of Nayarit

The motifs of the cross-stitch embroidery reveal pre-Hispanic and also European influences. The decorated hat is typical of this tribe. The men wear ear-rings, bracelets, rings, and belts with pockets, as well as a neckerchief.

show little or no foreign influence at all. So much for the local costumes. Apart from Yucatan, however, the visitor is only likely to see them at some of the big markets and festivals to which the people from the mountainous regions come down.

What other textiles are typical of the country and also form part of the outstanding achievements of Mexican folk-art? The sarape worn by the men, and the rebozo and, though somewhat rarer, the wrap-round skirt, the coloured, embroidered or woven belt (faja) and the "quexquemitl" worn by the women.

The Sarape

In the pre-Hispanic era the Indians of the mountainous regions wore a shawl or blanket made of cotton or other plant fibres, the "tilma". In those days a crude weaving device, which consisted of chains fastened to two wooden staves, was used. The upper stave was tied to a tree, whilst the lower one was fastened to the hips of the woman-weaver by means of a belt; the web was thus drawn tight by her weight. The shuttle was moved by hand. In some remote regions of the country the sarapes and also the huipiles and belts are still woven by this method.

The Spaniards introduced hand-looms and taught the Mexicans how to obtain and use wool. Blankets from Spain and from the North African coast no doubt served as models in teaching this craft to the native weavers, who apparently also copied the foreign designs. Wool is first said to have been woven in Apizaco in the state of Tlaxcala in 1540.

Sarape-weaving achieved its highest degree of excellence in the early 19th century. In those days sarapes of such outstanding and exquisite quality were produced that they satisfied even the most extravagant and elaborate tastes. True, the famous old sarapes of San Miguel Allende and Saltillo, with their ornate designs in vivid and harmonious colours, were not exactly comparable to Oriental carpets, but they nevertheless undoubtedly represented a notable achievement in the art of weaving. Nowadays the sarape is still an extremely popular garment that is worn in all parts of Mexico. Vivid colours are used sparingly, and the wool is usually woven in its

A Woman on the Market in Cuetzalan in the Sierra de Puebla

The head-dress made of thick strands of brown and purple wool and draped round the head in turban fashion is typical of this part of the country. As a rule the women wear two finely woven quexquemitls, – one over their shoulders, and the other folded together as an additional ornament over their head-dress.

various natural colours. Styles and designs vary from district to district and, in fact, from village to village, thus attesting to the great artistic creativeness of the weavers.

So far no detailed list of the different designs has been compiled, but one can say for certain that there are at least 200 to 300.

The finest sarapes are made in the state of Oaxaca (in particular in Teotitlan del Valle. In addition, there are about 40 villages where sarapes are also woven, mainly by the pre-Hispanic method.), in the state of Tlaxcala, namely in Santa Ana and the surrounding districts, in San Miguel Chiconcuac near Texcoco, not far from the capital, and in the states of Mexico and Michoacan. The sarapes worn by the Tarahumara Indians in the north of Mexico and by the Mayo Indians in the state of Sonora are of a particularly heavy quality but are not as well known as the sarapes woven in the above-mentioned districts. Very exquisite patterns are woven in some of the villages in the states of Guerrero and Mexico, above all in Coatepec de Harinas and Guadalupita; sarapes in these patterns can usually be seen at the markets in Taxco and Toluca, in Acaxochitlan in the state of Hidalgo, and in Ixcotla in the state of Tlaxcala. The sarapes in glaring colours, which can be bought in the tourist centres and which, so the tourist assumes, look like the genuine Mexican sarapes, have little connection with the folk-art of the country and are not worn by the native inhabitants.

According to the traditional custom of the various districts, the sarape is either woven as a blanket which is worn slung round the shoulders, or in a smaller size, with a slit in the middle through which to put one's head so that chest and back are covered.

The Rebozo

The rebozo is a long, narrow shawl which is chiefly used as a covering for the head. But it also serves as a means of carrying burdens and as a "pram". It is of foreign origin. There is however some controversy as to whether it is of Spanish or of Oriental origin, since there are countless regions in the world where the womenfolk work in the fields in the glaring sun and wear such a protective covering on their heads, which is designated by various names.

Chinanteca Indians attired in the Classical Pre-Hispanic Huipil

The women of this Indian tribe still wear the classical pre-Hispanic huipil, the designs and patterns of which show no foreign influence whatever. The material of the huipil and of the wrap-round skirt is hand-woven, and the designs are hand-embroidered.

The rebozo is usually made of silk, artificial silk, wool, or cotton, and occasionally, but rarely, of other plant fibres.

The finest rebozos are produced in three places, – in Tenancingo in the state of Mexico, in Santa Maria del Rio in the state of San Luis Potosi – a characteristic feature of the rebozos made here in former times was their dark green colour, a dye obtained from a special kind of moss, and in Jiquilpan in the state of Michoacan. The old technique of dyeing known as "ikat" is still used today even though chemical dyes are also used. The dyeing process consists of a number of stages. At first, the necessary number of warp threads into which the pattern, which is usually very ornate, is to be woven, are tied together and wrapped round with thread in those parts which are for the time being to remain undyed. The skeins are dipped in the dye solution and then dried. The parts that were wrapped round with thread are now untied, and those parts which have already been dyed are wrapped round with thread. In this way the undyed parts can now be dyed in a uniform colour or in various colours, by dipping them in the dye solutions. Since only about a dozen warp threads can be dyed at a time, one can well imagine the enormous amount of work that is involved in order to make a rebozo. The small irregularities in colouring which are unavoidable in this kind of work add to the attractive appearance of the rebozos.

Other well known types of shawls are the "ayates", or carrying-shawls, which are worn by the Otomi Indians of Hidalgo and Toluca and are made of an agave fibre (ixtle) and ornamented with an embroidered design, and the black rebozos with cross-stitch embroidery in bright colours, which are made in Hueyapan in the state of Puebla. Rebozos are also woven in the state of Oaxaca.

The Quexquemitl

This is a square shawl with a slit in the middle, through which one puts one's head. It was already worn in the pre-Hispanic era, and the name is of Aztec origin. The quexquemitl is still part of the local costume in the Sierra de Puebla and in a few other regions. The striking feature about the light, white quexquemitl of cotton that is worn in the Sierra de Puebla region is its woven pattern, whilst the heavier cotton quexquemitl of the

Indians on the Market in Huauchinango / Puebla, wearing Sarapes made in Acaxochitlan / Hidalgo

The sarapes they are wearing have a particularly striking design and have been woven in Acaxochitlan / Hidalgo.

Acaxochitlan district in the state of Hidalgo is distinguished by colourful cross-stitch embroidery in wool.

Other Textiles

Mention must also be made of various particularly fine materials which are used for skirts. In Acatlan near Chilapa in the state of Guerrero a heavy, black cotton material is woven, which is then embroidered with delightful flower and animal motifs in narrow strips. In Pinotepa and Jamiltepec in the state of Oaxaca, in the region not far from the border of the state of Guerrero and from the Pacific, heavy materials are woven, the threads of which are still dyed with indigo blue, with cochineal, and with a purple dye obtained from the purpura mollusc.

The ankle-length skirts and wrap-round skirts which are worn above all in the states of Puebla, Chiapas and Michoacan are usually tucked up round the hips by means of a belt made of material. This belt, the faja, is of pre-Hispanic origin. It is to be found in hundreds of varieties as regards length, width and design, and though it is one of the less noticeable forms of expression of Mexican folk-art, it is nevertheless an interesting one. In the above-mentioned states blouses made of linen are embroidered by hand with ornate designs. There is an extremely large variety of pleasing designs and many of them, like the "dirndl" dresses in Germany, have become popular far beyond the borders of their local district. Some of the designs in cross-stitch and beaded embroidery are most artistic.

The American Indian carries his provisions and other essential objects in a small bag when moving from place to place. As a rule these bags are made of ixtle or cotton fibres and are perfectly plain in style. The Otomi Indians, however, decorate their double-woven bags of wool and cotton with animal, flower and other ornamental designs. In the state of Hidalgo one frequently sees them busily engaged in spinning the threads.

Leatherwork

Primitive forms of leatherwork already existed in the pre-Hispanic era, but this craft also received many a new stimulus through the Spanish conquerors.

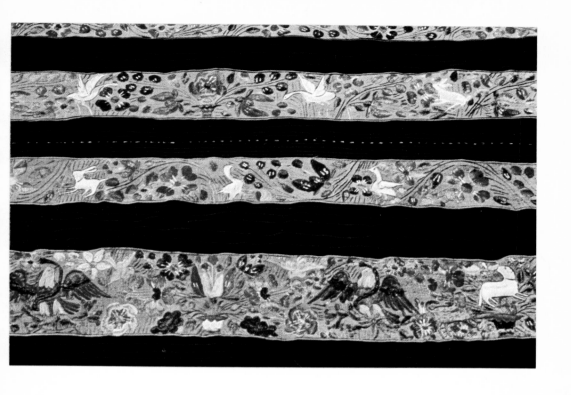

Hand-woven Skirt Material from Acatlan near Chilapa

The embroidered flower and animal motifs are typical of the materials woven in this district. The motif in the coat-of-arms of Mexico, the eagle catching a serpent, is also used.

Some of the Indian tribes prefer to go barefoot; those who do not, like the majority of the masses, wear leather-plaited sandals known as "huaraches". The Chamula Indians in Chiapas wear a peculiar type of sandal, which has a horn-shaped piece of leather attached to the heel and also a high protective leather covering over the wearer's heel.

In the region between the Pacific coast and Apatzingan in the state of Michoacan the cattle-breeders wear long raincoats made of suede, the style of which can no doubt be traced back to Spanish influences.

Ornate leatherwork is particularly in evidence on saddles and harnesses (see remarks on the "charreria", p. 60).

Glassware

In addition to the old Spanish techniques, French processes have also been used since the 19th century.

Nowadays drinking-glasses, carafes and other vessels are still manufactured in the small glass works in the capital, in Guadalajara and Puebla. The glass is of coarse quality, and the favourite colours used are brown, bluish purple, and green. Most of the objects are, however, artistically designed and find a ready market.

There are also various kinds of miniature glassware, especially those manufactured in Puebla, Mexico and Guadalajara, which are very exquisite. Perhaps their manufacture was prompted by a feeling of envy towards the miniature pottery ware – cups and bowls – made in Guanajuato, or perhaps it received its impetus solely from local artistic creativeness. But be that as it may, the glass-blowers began to make miniature coffee sets and four-branched candelabras about 2 inches high.

Metalwork

Although Mexico possesses huge deposits of various metals, some of which have still not been exploited, only a very crude method of obtaining copper and the use of silver and gold were known prior to the advent of the Spaniards. As can be seen from the Zapotec gold jewellery of Monte

Cross-stitch Embroidery on a Rebozo from Hueyapan / Puebla

Floral and animal designs are used and also scenes from everyday life.

Alban, now exhibited in the museum of Oaxaca, the goldsmith's craft, however, already reached a high degree of artistic perfection in early times.

The Spaniards first taught the Mexicans how to obtain and use iron and steel. Fine examples of wrought iron and steel work, which dates from the colonial period, can still be seen in the old towns of the states of Michoacan, Jalisco, Guanajuato and Oaxaca. The manufacture of branding-irons for cattle has survived longest. In Amozoc in the state of Puebla, buttons, buckles, and spurs, etc., are made of iron and decorated with small inlaid laminae of silver.

The typical knife of Mexico, which is usually long – and rarely curved – and resembles a dagger, is the "machete". Most of the Indians carry one on their person and use it as a tool for cutting or beating and also for self-defence, in which case it is a highly dangerous weapon when differences of opinion arise. Hand-wrought machetes of fine quality, especially those made in Oaxaca, are ornamented with engraved pictorial designs and mottoes.

Copper was already used for ornament prior to the advent of the Spaniards. Nowadays beautiful vessels of beaten copper are still made by primitive methods in Santa Clara del Cobre in the state of Michoacan. Sometimes these vessels are ornamented with pictorial scenes.

On the strength of a decree issued by Philip II in 1550, the Indians were forbidden to possess or to use precious metals. In order to be able to decorate their churches they now began to make candelabras, lamps and sacred vessels and, later, also jewellery out of tin. In the capital, in San Miguel Allende and Guanajuato, in Oaxaca and in some other places, this craft has survived up to the present day. During recent decades it has become the practice to paint designs on some of this tin-ware.

The tin masks made in various places are of more recent origin. They were first made about 1930. But since they have never been used as masks, they cannot be regarded as objects of the traditional folk-art.

As a result of the above-mentioned decree, silverware for religious and secular purposes was made exclusively by the immigrants, and European designs and styles served as models. Nor can the thriving manufacture of silver jewellery, mainly for tourists, which is today carried on above all in the capital, in Taxco and in other towns, be described as a branch of folk-art in the truest sense of the word. Some of this jewellery is copied from old pieces. But the Mexican silversmiths have also created unique, modern

34

Hand-woven Rebozos from Jiquilpan / Michoacan

The designs and patterns are similar to those used in Santa Maria del Valle / San Luis Potosi and in Tenancingo / Mexico. The extremely laborious dyeing process is described in detail on page 28.

designs. An exception – since it is based on older traditions – is the gold and silver filigree work of Tehuantepec, Tuxtla Gutierrez, Chiapas and Yucatan. The modern copies of the old silver jewellery made on the shores of Lake Patzcuaro are also noteworthy.

The "milagros" – hearts, figures, parts of the body, etc., varying in size from half an inch to two inches – are made of cast metal. They are hung near the pictures of saints as an offering for the healing of the part of the body concerned, for the procreation of offspring, or for protection from danger.

Until fairly recently a special kind of cross used to be made in Yalalag – and in earlier times in Choapan – in the mountainous region of the state of Oaxaca. Three smaller crosses were hung on both sides of it and a larger cross was suspended from the lower beam.

Precious Stones and other Jewellery

The ancient peoples of Mexico were masters of the art of working in hard stones, in particular obsidian and jade, as can be seen from the exhibits displayed in the museums. The modern copies of the images of the ancient deities and the agate-work manufactured in Puebla are in no way comparable to the achievements of earliest times. Nor can they be designated as genuine folk-art.

There is a flourishing gem-cutting industry in the state of Queretaro but it is of comparatively recent origin.

In those districts where the inhabitants still wear the local costume, chains are made of glass beads and different coloured seeds. The Huicholes make very lovely bracelets, chains and ear-rings of small glass beads (chaquira). But strange to say, these accessories are part of the local costume worn by the men.

In Yurequaro in the state of Michoacan, rosaries are made of seeds, and they were an important export article during the last war.

Wood

Furniture, church pews, church doors and statues carved of wood will not be dealt with at this point, since they come under the category of

Satchels used by the Otomi Indians, from the State of Hidalgo

This type of satchel is used in many parts of the country. It is worn almost exclusively by the men, who carry the usual utensils and provisions in it when they move from place to place. The patterns vary from district to district. Coloured ornamental embroidery is also used. The most unique and striking satchels are those used by the Otomi Indians.

colonial art. We should however like to mention various types of wooden wares which can be regarded as an essential part of Mexican folk-art.

In the district of Guadalajara a type of wicker chair with a leather seat and a back-rest is made, which, in Dr. Atl's opinion, is the only chair of its kind that dates back to the pre-Hispanic era in its origin. And this opinion would appear to be corroborated by the fact that the Huicholes use a similar type of chair for religious ceremonies. A rather unique type of chair with arm-rests and a high back-rest in the old style is still made in Apatzingan in the state of Michoacan; another typical but less ornate kind of chair is manufactured in Tacambaro.

In some of the states in the heart of Mexico painted wooden chairs in a plain style with a wickerwork seat are manufactured. They are very similar to the "farmhouse chairs" made in Europe in the 18th and 19th centuries.

There are so many different types of wooden chests – and their unique beauty lies in the various designs painted on them – that it is impossible to enumerate them in detail in this book. Wooden dolls are still carved by some tribes for religious purposes, but most of the dolls made only serve as toys. Walking-sticks with carved designs and painted in various colours – and sometimes the colours are rather too vivid – are made in Apizaco in the state of Tlaxcala.

In some states vessels and whisks (batidoras), used for stirring cocoa, are turned and carved. The most ornate stirring-spoons are made in the state of Michoacan.

The large wooden basins which are in use in various parts of the country nowadays are carved out of one block of wood, and fine cabinet woods are often used for this purpose. Though these utensils are of recent origin, they are, so to speak, indirectly descended from the old type of wash-tubs carved out of a single block of wood, which are still used in South Mexico.

Beautifully carved wares of light-coloured and relatively soft wood are made in the district round Lake Patzcuaro in the state of Michoacan. Tocoaro, a village on the lake, is known for its fishes carved of wood, and Sirahuen for its wooden spoons.

As striking examples of the "modern art" of wood-carving we should like to mention the exquisitely carved animals of the Sierra de Puebla region, in particular of San Pedro Totoltepec.

The Otomi Indians in the neighbourhood of Ixmiquilpan in the state of

A Mask from Acatlan / Puebla

The use of masks for folk-dances and tribal dances is a widespread custom not only in Mexico but also amongst other peoples. In this respect Mexico possesses an ancient tradition, for the earliest cultures there were already acquainted with such masks and with death masks, some of which are amongst the most valuable archaeological finds that have been discovered there. (Raul Kamffer Collection)

Hidalgo make wooden miniatures of instruments, which are ornamented with lavish inlaid designs in mother-of-pearl. On the market square of Tepoztlán in the state of Morelos the Indians offer wares carved out of bark, which are replicas of their huts and their villages in the mountains.

Until fairly recently it was the custom in the state of Veracruz to decorate the shells of coconuts with ornate carving. Cruder wares carved out of the rind of the jicara, a kind of gourd, are to be found in Jalpa de Mendez in the state of Tabasco and also in some of the villages of Oaxaca, above all in Pinotépa de Don Luis.

In various parts of the country, in particular in Oaxaca, bird-cages made out of small bamboo sticks are offered for sale on the markets. Some of these cages are extremely complicated structures, complete with turrets and oriels, and resemble fine villas. The bird-cages made by the Otomi Indians in the Valle Mezquital in the state of Hidalgo are replicas of the Cathedral of Mexico and can boast towers which are about 3 feet high.

Santa Maria del Rio in the state of San Luis Potosi is noted for its small wooden boxes ornamented with inlaid work. They are used as gift-boxes for rebozos. The inlaid work is, however, not as exquisite in style as it used to be in former times.

Wickerwork

Wickerwork is the predominating craft in all those parts of Mexico where palms and reeds grow in abundance. A typical piece of wickerwork is the "petate", a mat made of reeds, which in its origin dates from earliest times. It is used as a seat, as a table, or as a bed, and the patterns and style are the same everywhere. In San Pedro Totoltepec near Lerma in the state of Mexico reeds are used to make figures, seats and coloured mats. In Santa Ana in the state of Mexico clothes-baskets and chests are made out of dyed palm-leaves. This same material is also used in Tehuacan, the famous spa in the state of Puebla, to make various kinds of small figures, including mice and squirrels which are about half an inch long. In Tzintzuntzan in the state of Michoacan, angels and crucifixes are made of plaited straw. Here, too, stylized figures which are broad in shape and are used to fan and kindle the fire are produced. The above-mentioned materials and also maize fibres are used to make dolls.

A Painted Wedding-chest from Quiroga / Michoacan

The inscription on this chest is: "Lend me to no one, give me to no one, for I am yours for ever."

Crude rain-capes are made of plaited reeds in some parts of the country. The loose parts are worn on the outside. In some of the more remote and rainy districts one frequently sees this type of rain-cape with beautiful plaited work on the inside.

The Sombrero

If one sees a man without a hat in any of the rural districts, one can assume for certain that he is not a Mexican. Hat-plaiting – usually of palm-leaves – is extremely widespread. The above-mentioned places which specialize in wickerwork also make hats. In Nacahuca in the state of Tabasco reeds and sugar-canes are also used to make hats. In Becal in the state of Campeche hats of "panama quality", some of which are exported, are plaited of particularly fine palm-leaves. In San Francisco del Rincón near León in the state of Guanajuato almost the entire population is employed in plaiting sombreros. This domestic industry was introduced by Spanish monks and, strange to say, has survived in this village, which is situated on a high plateau, in spite of the fact that the raw materials have to be transported from the Pacific and the Gulf coast, – certainly a difficult matter in former times. Nowadays the hats made here are sold in almost every part of the country.

Some of the Indian tribes, as for instance the Chamulas, wear ornaments on their hats. The manner in which their hats are draped with long, narrow and coloured silk ribbons indicates whether they are married or single. The Huicholes decorate the upper part of their hats with embroidered crosses or strips of red wool. In former times they used to fasten butterfly pupae or red tassels to the brim, but nowadays they use narrow strips cut out of coloured match-boxes and even out of pill-boxes instead.

Baskets and Hammocks

An entire book could be written about Mexican baskets alone, since they are to be found in so many different varieties. The baskets offered for sale on the market of Oaxaca are of especially fine quality. In San Juan del

Lacquer-work from Uruapan / Michoacan

On a sarape from Nahuatzen, in the top left-hand corner, a dish made from
the rind of the jicara, a kind of gourd, and on the right, a wooden platter. The
lacquer-work of Uruapan is decorated with a lively but stylized floral design. The
objects are first of all covered with a plain lacquer. The surface is then scraped
so as to make small hollows for the ornamental design. These hollows are then
filled with the other coloured lacquers. The more skilfully this work is executed,
the smoother and more symmetrical the appearance of the entire surface. A special
technique in applying the lacquer makes the surface resistant.

Rio in the state of Gueretaro animal figures and coloured baskets are plaited of fine twigs. Tequisquiapan in particular, which is nearby, spezializes in this craft.

In Tlaxiaco, a mountain village of the Mixteca alta in the state of Oaxaca – a district which in parts reminds one of the Black Forest – one can watch the Indians plaiting panniers of palm-leaves; they carry these baskets on their heads by means of a thong over their forehead. Tiny baskets the size of a fingernail are sold on the market in Guanajuato.

In the tropical coastal regions people sleep in hammocks. Even the wealthy use them, though they may have beds for the cooler season. Anyone who has become accustomed to a hammock will undoubtedly prefer it to a bed during hot nights. The plainer type of hammock is made of maguey or henequén (kinds of agave plants) fibres, the more elaborate type of cotton fibres. And incidentally, there are double hammocks, just as there are double beds!

Stoneware

Two household utensils made of stone are essential requisites of every Mexican kitchen, – the metate and the stone mortar. The metate is a three or four-legged stone slab with a slightly concave surface, on which maize is ground and crushed by means of a stone roller. The tortillas, or flat maize cakes, which in Mexico are eaten as a substitute for potatoes and bread, are made of this maize pulp.

Chili and other spices used in preparing the highly seasoned sauces which are typical of the Mexican cuisine, are crushed in the stone mortar (Spanish "molcajete", Aztec "tamolote"). In some districts the metates are decorated with brightly coloured painted designs.

Horn, Tortoise-shell and Bone

In the district of Toluca, namely in San Antonio la Isla, and in Oaxaca combs are carved out of horn. The handles are usually carved in the shape of animals, for instance fishes, or a horse's head. Knitting needles and

Wickerwork of Reeds, Straw and Palm-leaves

On a sarape from Teotitlan del Valle / Oaxaca, in the back row, a hunter from Tehuacan / Puebla, an angel from Tzintzuntzan – this is a variety of fan, as represented by the skirt of the figure, – and a horseman from Lerma / Mexico. In the middle row: a child's rattle shaped like a bird, from the Valle de Mexquital / Hidalgo, and on the right, a horseman from Tehuacan. In the front row: a small basket from Oaxaca, and a bird, with movable wings, made of straw. The Indians sell these birds, which are probably harder to make than any of the other wares shown here, to each other for the mere sum of 20 centavos, that is to say less than a penny.

chessmen are made in Paracho in the state of Michoacan. Along the Gulf coast tortoise-shell is used to make combs, small trinkets and miniature figures of animals.

In some districts small square laminae, used for winding thread, are carved of bone and sometimes of wood. Some of them are decorated with simple designs, others with miniatures. In Paracho in the state of Michoacan, bone is also used to make chessmen and other small objects.

Paper and Printing

The ancient peoples of Mexico were already acquainted with the primitive process of making paper. And coarse paper is still produced by means of this old technique in the Sierra de Puebla and used for magic purposes. The colour of the crude human figures depicted on the paper indicates the purpose for which it is intended: light-coloured paper is used as a magic love-spell, darker paper in order to exorcise illness, and dark brown paper for black magic.

The above example is no doubt the clearest proof that the visitor to Mexico can find anything and everything there, – from ultra-modern skyscrapers to customs which date from the earliest times of mankind.

Another custom which prevails in the Sierra de Puebla is that of cutting the figures of deities out of tissue-paper. These figures are then buried in the fields in order to ensure a good harvest. According to what has been planted, these paper deities are depicted as carrying either tomatoes, chili, maize, or beans in their hands.

In some of the villages close to the extinct volcano of Ajusco, not far from the capital, paper pictures are made by punching small piles of tissue-paper. These pictures are placed on the graves in the village cemeteries during the night of All Souls. The motifs are in keeping with the occasion and depict the relatives of the departed in the act of setting out food and a jug of pulque (fermented agave sap) for their dead. According to an old belief, the dead return to the living once a year, during the night of All Souls. The souls of the departed are refreshed with food and drink, and the living then partake of the remains of the offerings which they have placed on the graves.

46

A Vendor making Piñatas

During the last few weeks before Christmas earthenware pitchers are decorated with tissue-paper and silver-paper and transformed into animals or stars. The pitcher is then filled with sweetmeats, nuts, fruit and chocolate. During the festivities which are held shortly before Christmas, young and old alike "beat the piñata" with their eyes blindfolded. No such festivity would be complete without the observance of this old custom.

In many villages large sheets of tissue-paper are cut or punched in the shape of various designs, flowers or animals, to mark the occasion of festivities. Puebla, Toluca, Tlaxcala and Texcoco are noted for this craft, but the most exquisite decorations of this kind are to be found in the district near Molango, in the mountainous region of the state of Hidalgo.

The craftsmanship of some of the small printing works in Mexico might well be designated as a branch of folk-art, for they print beautiful, ornamental placards and handbills for festivals and other special occasions. But unfortunately this custom now appears to be gradually dying out.

Lacquer-work

The assumption that the Chinese art of lacquering influenced this Mexican craft cannot be definitely accepted as an established fact, even though there is a certain similarity between the technique used and the early practice of obtaining lacquer from caterpillars. But on the strength of the research conducted by various writers and the remains of pre-Hispanic lacquer ware which have come to light in the course of archaeological excavations, it would appear that this craft originated in Mexico itself. Nowadays chemical lacquers are used almost exclusively, and the quality of the wares produced has deteriorated alarmingly during recent years owing to the increasing demand of the souvenir trade. In spite of this fact, however, there are still a few craftsmen who, either for the sake of tradition or because they enjoy the support of some patron or other, still adhere faithfully to the old styles.

Lacquer ware is still made today in Uruapan, Quiroga and Patzcuaro in the state of Michoacan, in Chiapa de Corzo in the state of Chiapas, and in Olinalá in the mountains of Guerrero. In Peribán in the state of Michoacan this craft ceased to exist at the beginning of this century. Uruapan, Quiroga and Olinalá are noted for their painted and lacquered chests. In all the above-mentioned places dishes carved out of the rind of gourds and flat wooden dishes are lacquered and decorated with designs consisting of flower and animal motifs. The style and technique vary from village to village; some of the designs are overlaid, others are painted on the surface of the object in question.

48

Wares made of Tin, Wax, Paper and Confectionery

The candlesticks made of tin and the surrounding ornamentation in wax are made in Santa Maria del Rio / San Luis Potosi. Over the candlestick on the left there is a replica of the Basilica of the Virgin of Guadalupe, over the one on the right, the replica of another building. In the background, ornamental designs cut out of coloured tissue-paper, which are used as decorations at festivals. In the foreground, a death's-head made of icing. A Christian name is inscribed on its forehead. On All Souls Day people give each other these death's-heads as a present in order to remind José, Josephine, or whatever their name may be, that they, too, will one day go the same way. (The Museum of San Luis Potosi)

Painting

The cathedrals dedicated to the most important Mexican saints, as for instance the Basilica of the Virgin of Guadalupe and those in Chalma and San Juan de los Lagos, contain countless votive pictures. Most of the scenes, which are painted in oil on metal panels, depict the healing of sickness or the rescue from danger. There is an inscription referring to the occasion in question on many of them. Some obscure painter or other is commissioned to paint these "retablos" by the person who has been healed or saved and they are then dedicated to the saint in question as an offering of gratitude.

Images of the Madonna made out of Seeds

As a result, no doubt, of European influences, images of the Madonna are still made out of small seeds, which are glued together, in some parts of Mexico. The face of the Madonna is usually painted on a small ivory lamina.

Wax Ware

The ancient peoples of Mexico already practised the craft of bee-keeping and it can thus be assumed that they knew how to obtain wax. Puebla was known for the wax dolls made there. In some districts the wax-moulders embellish candles with ornate floral decorations. Santa Maria del Rio and San Luis Potosi are famed for the exquisite wax filigree-work produced there, as for instance replicas of the Basilica of the Virgin of Guadalupe, the national saint of Mexico.

Masks

The Mexican masks can be traced back in their origin to ancient traditions. There are some fine collections of masks made of clay, stone, obsidian and jade, some of them decorated with inlaid work, others of priceless value, to be seen in the various museums of the country.

Toy Horses made of Papier Mâché

Papier mâché is used to make carnival masks and toy animals. It is also used above all for the "Judas" images, which are part of the customs observed at Easter. Fireworks are tied to these figures and they are set on fire on Easter Saturday. Some of these "Judas" images are twice as large as life-size. They represent anonymous persons, death, and also well-known personalities who are, however, disliked.

Most of the papier mâché wares are made in the capital and in Celaya.

Today masks are still worn for many of the local folk-dances as well as for some of the tribal dances, as for instance the Yuaquis in the north of Mexico. Most of these masks are made of wood and painted; in some districts they are grotesquely decorated with animals' teeth, antlers, hides and skins. Almost all the masks still known today are made in the states of Michoacan, Guerrero, Puebla, Oaxaca and Sonora.

In other districts, especially in Celaya and other villages in the state of Guanajuato, masks are made of papier mâché and painted in glaring colours. As in the case of the clay masks, the technique used can be traced back to ancient traditions. The papier mâché masks are moulded in clay masks. Since the latter are constantly in use, they sometimes break. The result is a negative mask, in which the positive mask needed for production is then pressed and moulded.

Musical Instruments

Of the instruments used in the pre-Hispanic era, some types of drums are still used and made by certain remote tribes, who also make small fiddles and guitars, – instruments which the Spaniards introduced into the country, for in earliest times stringed instruments were unknown in Mexico. The more elaborate stringed instruments are manufactured in Paracho in the state of Michoacan, and the marimbas, a kind of xylophone, are made in the state of Chiapas.

Toys and Miniatures

The manufacture of toys and miniatures is so manifold and interesting that it is the only subject so far on which a detailed compilation has been made. Every branch of Mexican folk-art has its own toys and miniatures of its particular wares. Wax dolls, marionettes and rag-dolls are still manufactured today, even though the demand for them has decreased considerably as a result of the production of articles made of plastics.

Miniatures

The inventiveness and perseverance of the Mexicans in creating these miniatures is inexhaustible. The candlestick and coffee set made of glass are from Puebla. In the centre, a "charro" of earthenware in half a walnut, from Amozoc / Puebla. The open walnuts, which contain a wedding scene, a bullfight, or a group of singers (the famous mariachis from Jalisco), have been carved in the prison in Guanajuato. The cigarette — of normal size — gives one an idea of the minute size of these wares.

Artificial fruits which are carved out of wood and are painted and varnished so skilfully that they appear to be real are made in Uruapan. Papantla in the state of Veracruz is noted for its delightful little baskets, crocodiles and scorpions plaited of vanilla stems.

Thin strands are kneaded out of chicle, the basis of chewing gum, and plaited together to make little baskets, figures of animals and also greetings cards. Tenosique in the state of Tabasco is the home of chicle-work. In 1958 such wares were also made in Campeche, but by 1960 they had disappeared from the market since the cultivation of chicle has decreased very considerably. Small objects and figures of the Madonna are, however, still made of chilte, a sap which is similar to chicle, in Talpa de Allende in the mountainous region of the state of Jalisco.

In various prisons throughout the country the prisoners make different kinds of miniatures, as for instance small pistols. The prison in Guanajuato is noted for the carved walnuts made there, which open to reveal a wedding, a bullfight, or a group of mariachis, the singers of folksongs who are famed throughout the entire country.

Miniatures are also made elsewhere, as for example in Amozoc in the state of Puebla, where tiny market scenes are moulded out of clay. The turkeys – a bird that is a native of Mexico but is known all over the world – in these miniatures are only about one-tenth of an inch high. Miniatures depicting groups of singers and bullfight scenes and fashioned out of wire and clay are made in Quiroga in the state of Michoacan.

Featherwork

The highly artistic craft of making royal robes out of the coloured feathers of tropical birds gradually died out after Mexico was conquered by the Spaniards. For some time, thanks to the influence of missionaries, religious pictures continued to be made in featherwork, but these were eventually superseded by more worldly and romantic pictures in the 17th and 18th centuries.

The last examples of this craft, which is now completely extinct, were greetings cards depicting birds in the 1920's.

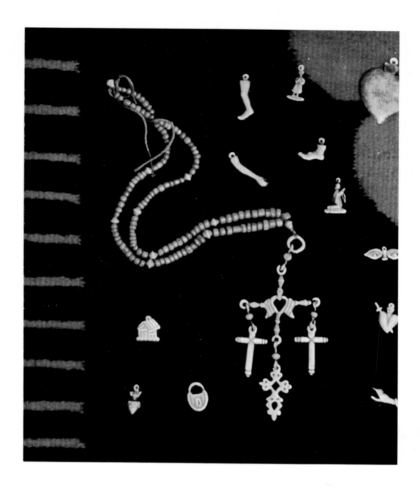

Silverware

On a sarape from Teotitlan del Valle / Oaxaca, a "cross of Yalalag" from the mountainous region of Oaxaca, and various milagros either cast of silver or fashioned out of silver-leaf. The shape of the milagros, which are hung near the picture of a saint, indicates what the person who has made the offering wishes for: the healing of some complaint, many offspring, or the protection of his property and possessions. They are also hung up as a thanks offering. Pictures of the chief saints are often surrounded by hundreds of milagros.

The Mexicans are profoundly conscious of the ties of blood and friend-ship. And perhaps this is one of the reasons why every fiesta is a special occasion to them. Certain festive occasions have inspired Mexican folk-art to such an extent that it seems fitting to mention them in some detail.

On Palm Sunday artistically plaited palm branches are sold in front of the churches. They are then blessed by the priest in the church and are taken home by those who have bought them. In hundreds of villages the Indians still perform their own passion plays. On Maundy Thursday and Good Friday – in particular in the capital – "Judas" images are sold, which are made of twigs and papier mâché and vary in size from a couple of inches to figures which are larger than life-size. These images may represent skeletons, some person or other, prominent persons in the history of the country, or grotesque devils. The larger figures are filled with fireworks and on Easter Saturday are either burnt or blown up.

Like the Chinese, the Mexicans have developed pyrotechnics to a high degree of excellence. Every fiesta must close with a display of "cohetes", rockets and other fireworks. Whether the fireworks consist of ordinary rockets, or of artistically built structures in the shape of animals, walls or houses and decorated with Catherine-wheels, this is always the big attraction of the fiesta. Some of these structures are 15, 25 and 30 feet high. The "toritos", dummies of bulls made of bamboo canes, papier mâché, or raffia mats, are particularly imposing. Above the body of the bull, which is about 3 feet long and nearly 2 feet high, there is a structure, 3 to 6 feet high, made of bamboo canes, to which Catherine-wheels and rockets are fastened. The "bull-dancer" – originally this was in all probability a dance to invoke fertility – carries the bull and the entire structure on his shoulders. The fireworks then go off with a terrific din, and the body of the bull protects the bearer from getting burnt. In those districts where this dance no longer has a serious, ritual character, the young people of the village run after the dancer in order to snatch parts of the bull whilst the fireworks are exploding. And it goes without saying that the most boisterous and daring young men frequently sustain burns.

We have already mentioned the custom which is observed on All Souls night. The fact must be stressed that the Mexicans are on a more familiar

Wares of Wood and Chicle

In a shallow wooden tub, carved in one piece, such as the Indian women in the mountains of Chiapas use for washing clothes, there are a whisk from Paracho and a wooden fish from Tocoaro, both in the state of Michoacan. The small flower-basket is made of chicle, the basis of chewing gum, and has been fashioned after the chicle strands have been dyed. The vessels made out of the rinds of gourds were carved in Tabasco. The wares are displayed on a sarape from Guerrero.

footing, as it were, with death than any other peoples in the world. In their folk-art we find death depicted in many forms: as a marionette, as clay figures, and in pictures. The bakeries bake "death bread". The confectioners make ornate death's-heads of icing. In Toluca toys are made which represent coffins, out of which a corpse bobs up when the lid is opened. Another extremely popular depiction of death is the funeral procession, complete with open coffin, which is mounted on scissors so that one can set the procession in motion.

In the form of the "calaveras" the prominent persons and events of the year are commented on and also symbolized by skeletons in both drawings and print. Many of these descriptions remind one of the ballads of the minstrels in olden days.

Another festival that is typical of Mexico is the posada, which is celebrated a few days before Christmas Eve. The fate of the Holy Family on their search for lodgings (posada) in Bethlehem is enacted in song. Finally, the "piñata" is beaten. This is a vessel made of clay in the form of a donkey, lamb or star and beautifully decorated with crimped and silver paper. During the last few weeks before Christmas one can see piles of these vessels on all the markets, where the vendors are busily engaged in transforming them into "piñatas" with great artistic skill.

In many parts of Mexico special customs are observed on Ascension Day. In the capital small figures of donkeys made of twigs, maize stalks and clay are sold in front of the churches. Little boxes of flowers, fruits and sweetmeats are suspended from their backs.

RITUAL ART

The Huicholes, an Indian tribe in the mountainous region of Nayarit, contribute an important share to this branch of Mexican folk-art. For some of the rituals in their religious cult they make arrows decorated with eagle's feathers. In order to win the favour of their deities the children make offerings of "god's eyes", sticks bound together in the form of a cross and decorated at each end with squares woven of bright red wool. They also ornament the rinds of gourds with small glass beads (chaquira) in the form of allegorical designs or animal motifs.

Votive Tablets and Magic Paper

On a mat made of reeds, in the upper row, a votive tablet expressing gratitude to the Virgin of Guadalupe for the healing of a serious disease, a greetings card of the year 1930, one of the last examples of featherwork, and a figure made of amatl, a coarse paper still produced by means of an old technique in the Sierra de Puebla and used for black magic. In the lower row, a votive tablet made by the Huichol Indians, on which they ask their deities for a successful hunt, and a figure made of tissue-paper as an offering for a good tomato crop, from the Sierra de Puebla.

The Huicholes also make strange and fascinating votive tablets, which depict requests to their gods: for instance, for a successful hunt, for a good harvest, for rain, and so on. With the aid of a tropical wax they glue these pictures, which are made of threads of wool, to thin sheets of wood. There is a primitive creativeness about these tablets, which reminds one of the drawings of animals in the caves of the Stone Age or in modern art. But their sense of colour can certainly vie with the vehement paintings of our modern era.

CHARRERIA / HORSEMANSHIP

Horses were first introduced into Mexico by the Spaniards. Today the Mexicans rank amongst the best equestrians in the world. The old traditions are still fostered and observed in the "charro" clubs. The word "charro" cannot be adequately translated by "cowboy", for as in former times, so also today, many of the big landowners and members of the aristocracy belong to the exclusive riding clubs of the "charros". The outward and visible signs of the "charro" are the tight-fitting riding dress of leather or material, which is decorated with silver ornamentation, and the broad-brimmed sombrero. The silver ornamentation, spurs, harnesses and saddles are often extremely ornate and costly. And the manufacture of these articles plays an important part in the folk-art of the country. Special features in this respect are the exquisite leatherwork with embossed ornamentation, and the spurs, stirrups and other accessories wrought in silver.

MARKETS

The markets held on set days in the week and those which mark the occasion of some special festival often present the best opportunity to buy objects of Mexican folk-art. Nowadays, unfortunately, one has to go to the more remote districts if one wishes to see a genuine Indian market. But even in the urban markets which have been modernized to a considerable extent,

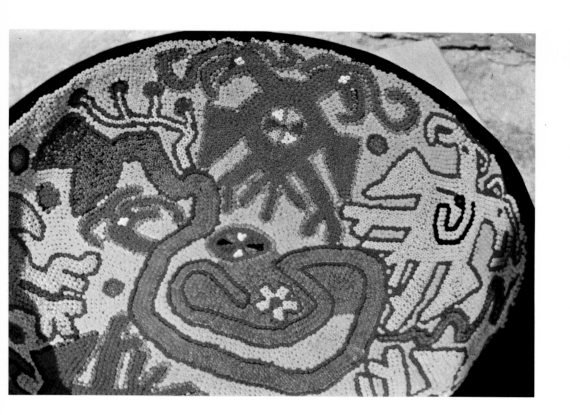

Chaquira (Glass Beads) Receptacle made by the Huichol Indians

The Huichol Indians put a kind of resin not only on their votive tablets but also on the inside of the receptacles which they carve out of the rinds of gourds. They then stick small, coloured glass beads on this resin. These receptacles are only used for some of the rituals in their religious cult. Glass beads were only introduced into Mexico fairly late in its history. But the motif depicted here is very old and particularly interesting. In the foreground, a snake, the phallic symbol of early primitive religions, behind it – a plant, symbolizing the tree of life, or the maize-stalk, a widespread symbol in Mexico. The eagle is regarded by the Huicholes as sacred. Double-headed it stands for "the eagle that looks in every direction".

the observant visitor will notice one feature which is typical of the genuine Indian markets, too, — namely the atmosphere of tranquillity which prevails. There is no raucous shouting; in fact, there is no loud talking at all, and laughter is always subdued. Business is conducted in a peaceful, quiet way.

In the capital and other large towns markets are held every day. The following list gives the most important markets and the set days on which they are held.

Charro Saddle and Harness

The charros are crazy about horses and riding. "Cowboy" is by no means an adequate translation of the word "charro". The charros foster the old equestrian traditions which were formerly observed on the haciendas, the large estates in Mexico. A special branch of Mexican folk-art continues to flourish as a result of the charros' desire for unique and costly riding accessories: finely woven sarapes, beautiful, ornate leatherwork, and exquisitely engraved silver accessories, like those shown in our picture, represent a value which is equivalent to that of a luxury car.

Like a burning-glass that converges the sun's rays,
each volume of the
METROPOLIS BOOKS
focusses the various aspects of a theme so that
they form a unity.

Titles available in this series

Pierre Schmidt
OLD MASTERS IN COLMAR
Grünewald and Schongauer in Colmar
64 pages with 28 colour plates. Cloth-binding.

The works of the Old Masters are especially impressive
for their creation was prompted by a deep religious
faith, and it is this quality in them which profoundly
moves the beholder even today. In addition to other
works of art, Schongauer's masterpieces and, above all,
Grünewald's Isenheim Altar are the theme of this book.

Carl Pospesch and Hans Thür
SALZBURG AND ITS FESTIVAL
64 pages with 28 colour plates. Cloth-binding.

This volume, with an Introduction by Hans Thür, has
as its subject the town of Salzburg, both as the scene
of the Festivals and also as a centre of ancient culture.
The colour plates by Carl Pospesch do not merely
serve to illustrate the text but are in themselves a unique
masterpiece.